Upstream

by
KRISTINE O'CONNELL GEORGE

illustrated by **DEBBIE TILLEY**

Houghton Mifflin Harcourt
Boston New York

For information about permission to reproduce
selections from this book, write to
trade.permissions@hmhco.com or to Permissions,
Houghton Mifflin Harcourt Publishing Company,
3 Park Avenue, 19th Floor, New York, New York 10016.

hmhco.com

The text was set in 14-point Beo Sans.
The illustrations were executed in pen and ink.

The Library of Congress has cataloged the hardcover
edition as follows:
George, Kristine O'Connell.
Swimming upstream : middle school poems /
by Kristine O'Connell George.
p. cm.
Summary: A collection of poems capture the feelings
and experiences of a girl in middle school.
1. Middle school students—Juvenile poetry. 2. Middle
schools—Juvenile poetry. 3. Children's poetry,
American. 4. Girls—Juvenile poetry. [1. Schools—
Poetry. 2. American poetry.] I. Title.
PS3557.E488 S95 2002
811'.54—dc21
2002002746

ISBN: 978-0-618-15250-6 hardcover
ISBN: 978-1-328-90018-0 paperback

Manufactured in the United States
DOC 10 9 8 7 6 5 4 3 2 1
4500698282

FOR DINAH STEVENSON

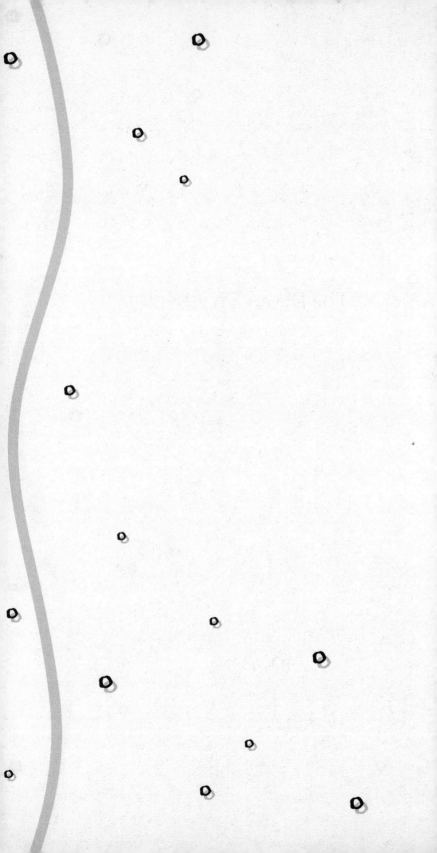

Many, many thanks to Judi Craven, M.S., Counselor, Lindero Canyon Middle School, Agoura, Calif.; Suzanne Peterson, Librarian, Santa Monica-Malibu Unified School District; Ashley Bravin and Courtney Elizabeth George, current and former middle schoolers; as well as Alice Schertle and Lynne T. Whaley, fellow authors and dear friends. Your insightful readings of the early versions and the reams of encouragement and support were greatly appreciated. All of you helped to keep me afloat while I was swimming upstream!

Wake-up Call

September morning, still remembering
last night's strange dream—
lost in an endless corridor,
opening a single door,
finding dozens more,
not knowing
where
I'm going.

Before School

I spot them in the crowd,
three familiar faces from elementary school—
    Sumako got braces!
    Ryan is so much taller.
    Zach looks just the same.

The warning bell rings,
everyone scatters,
    each of us going
    our separate ways.

Locker

I've got your numbers.
Twelve ... eleven ... twenty-one.
Why won't you open?

Lost

The morning nightmare.
Lost and too afraid to ask,
Where do I belong?

Late

The final bell rings,
long hallway—hollow, empty—
my footsteps too loud.

Homeroom

I find the right room—
head for the last row, keeping
my back to the wall.

Identity

The fill-in-the-blank question
     on the form Ms. Pierson
     passed out reads:
     What would you like to be called?

The other kids have turned in their forms.
     I'm still thinking,
     chewing my pencil,
     trying on new names.

Changing Classes

As soon as the bell rings,
students pour out the doors,
surging down the halls,
shoving, jostling, dodging,
in a roar of voices.

Pushing forward, I weave
in, out, and among
a thousand others,
feeling as if
            I'm swimming upstream.

My Locker

I spin the dial,
lift the latch,
a space all my own
in this crazy place.
I linger,
consider
crawling inside,
closing the door
behind me,
spending the day
watching
the world pass
            between
                        these
                                    narrow
                                            slats.

Which Lunch Table?

Where do I sit?
All my friends
from last year
have changed;
my world is
    f r a c t u r e d ,
    l o p s i d e d ,
    r e a r r a n g e d .

Where do I fit?
Nothing is clear.
Can already tell
this will be
a jigsaw year.

Margo

I helped Margo
>with buttons in second grade,
>skating and soccer in third,
>explained jokes over and over
>so Margo could laugh, too.
>Margo, slower than the rest of us,
>counted on me to wait,
>to help her catch up.
>Depended on me
>to pull her along,
>to help her belong.

Now I see Margo
>at the edge of a crowd,
>looking more than lost.
>She doesn't see me wave.
>We're in different classes,
>I'm going places
>Margo can't find.
>Margo. Margo
>falling farther
>and farther
>behind.

School I.D. Card

Is my nose
    that big?
My hair
    so haystacky?
My neck
    that long?
Everyone else's
    looks fine.
So why is mine
    all wrong?

Kori

Something about this girl's grin
looks familiar. She calls out,

> *Wait! I think I know you.*
> *What school did you go to?*

> I know you, too! Weren't we
> in second grade together?

> *You had a frog umbrella?*

> You could hang a spoon
> from your nose?

It's Kori!
My old friend—
    my moved-away
    lost-track
    moved-back
    maybe new
    old friend.

New Friends Talking

Talking all the way, we're suddenly at my house.
We're not done, so much more to talk about,
so we turn around, keep on walking and talking
all the way back to Kori's house, but we're *still* not
finished, so we walk around the park (twice), then we
keep walking and talking halfway back to my house.
Then,

> we run straight home
> to phone.

Band

Mr. McKagan introduced
trumpet and percussion.
We met saxophone,
clarinet, and oboe.
Now we get
to choose.

I will be flute,
Ryan trombone,
and Craig is in love
with tuba,
that deep, bronze,
wide, round,
mellow, maroon
tuba sound.

Each Class

Each class
 a new textbook.

Each class
 You are not babies,
 this is not elementary school,
 we expect more of you.

Each class
 homework assigned.

Heading home—
 staggering past Zach,
 both of us
 with 100 pounds
 of school
 on our backs.

New Flute

Lips stretched out of shape
after blowing and blowing.
This flute is broken.

Shy

Pass me in the hall
    glance my way
    tease me a little
    tease me a lot

or even just say my name.

Guaranteed,
    won't take much—
            I blush.

Math

    5
    5 squared
    5 to the second power

Mrs. Bollo hands back my math quiz
    doom
    doom squared
    doom to the second power

Mrs. Bollo explains, making it clear—
says, "I'm glad you're in my class this year.
Your work shows potential."
    Happiness
    Happiness squared
    Happiness exponential!

The Other Me

The other me knows what to wear,
fits in, doesn't stick out,
is one of them.

The other me remembers jokes,
doesn't get teased
by anyone.

The other me doesn't have big feet,
doesn't stumble,
doesn't drop her lunch tray.

So, where *is* she,
this amazing
Other Me?

Dressing for P.E.

No privacy in the locker room!
I Houdini out of my sweatshirt.
Snap a quick towel flip.
Reverse.
Finish with a flourish.

The Trick:
Changing in and out of gym clothes
so not one square inch of skin shows.

Gossip

Whispers,
sly looks,
            notes slipped
into books.

I look away—
don't need
to see
to know
            those notes
are all
about me.

Flute Practice

After much practice,
flute still suffers severe case
of laryngitis.

Group

Kori and I have blended
        into a new group:
                Kori and me,
                Jaleesa from Kenya,
                Lupe from Mexico,
                Jaz from France,
                Sumako from Arkansas.
Friday night is our first official
                United Nations Slumber Party.

Hall Pass

Guess they don't want to
     misplace one of us,
have to confess to our parents
     one of us escaped.
So if you need to go to the
     cafeteria, office, library,
     restroom, or whatever,
you're expected to haul
     a weathered hunk of lumber
     huge as a rowboat oar.

Only one way to leave class—
     rowing down these wide halls
     with this enormous pass.

School Librarian

Mrs. Thompson knows I love sad stories.
The books she lends me
come with
hidden bookmarks—

folded tissues tucked into
the sad parts.

Costume Day

Jaz wears a sari,
Zach is a plunger (don't ask),
Ryan comes as a corpse.
I'm an alien (again)
with aluminum foil.

Kori's wings are so wide
we have to help her
through the doors.
Best, since we all
passed the quiz,
Mrs. Bollo keeps her promise

and we get to
wrap her up
like a mummy
in toilet paper.

New Shoes

My heart leaps
as Shoe Salesperson
appears from behind
the curtain
with a stack
of boxes!
I'm singing inside:

>   *They've got my size!*
>   *They've got my size!*

Shoe Salesperson kneels
in front of me,
lifts the lid . . .

>   "I thought you might like *These.*"

Pointing at Kori's and Lupe's shoes,
I explain:

>   "I want *Those.*"

Shoe Salesperson sneers:
>   "They don't make *Those*
>   in *your* size."

So that is how I ended up with
>   *These.*

Is It Monday Again?

Who decided to divide Time
    into seven square pieces
    (five for school, two for me)
    on these calendar pages?
Who decided to divide Time,
    with her countless ages,
    and lock her up
    in these little paper cages?

Pole Song

Monday morning, waiting for the bus,
the older kids laugh at the little boy
    who's leaning against
    the metal light pole,
    his ear held close,
    eyes shut.

They haven't a clue, yet I know.
    (It's something I used to do.)
    I'm remembering the sharp smell
    of cold metal as he taps a nickel
    against the hollow pole, listening
    to what only he can hear—

    those long, old air songs
    as his tall steel bell rings
    with the secret music
    a metal pole sings.

Pop Quiz

Mr. Shirling snaps
our graded tests
face-down
on our desks.

Kori flips her paper up,
gets it over with,
like a quick rip
of a Band-Aid.

I'll wait until I'm ready,
ready to know,
then I'll peel my test up,
        slow, slow, slow.

S N O B

Scanning the crowd,
Noticing
Only the other
sno**B**s

Staring right through me
Never thinking
ab**O**ut
any**B**ody else.

Stuck up
Narrow
Obnoxious
Boring

Someone
No one
Ought to
Bother knowing.

Lunch Survey

We open our paper bags:

Peanut butter plain
Peanut butter tortilla
Peanut butter pita
P B & J
P B & mayo
P B & banana
P B & pickles

Zach lifts the lid of his
insulated aluminum lunch box:
sushi.

Long Jump

Brittany and Jaleesa cheering,
I run as hard as I can,
        focusing
far beyond the sandpit.

I leap, hold air,
pull with my fingertips,
land solid,

weight forward,
and know

        I can do anything.

All I need

        is a running start.

More Flute Practice

At long last, my breath
and this silver tube create
a few flutelike notes.

So Much Better Than I Expected

Today

> enough hot water for a shower
> a better grade than I expected
> a certain someone noticed me
> peanut butter and pickles for lunch
> social studies report postponed (whew!)
> I finally won a tennis match
> 6–0 6–4
> macaroni and cheese for dinner
> no homework
> six phone calls
> five e-mails
> one snail mail
> a great library book for later

a perfect, straight-set, levitate-off-the-planet day.

Band Practice

Somehow, Ryan
	misjudges
the length
	of his slide,
knocking over
	his music stand,
which hits Sumako
	on the head.
Three more stands
	clatter down
before Ryan tames
	his trombone.

Sumako is fine.
	Mr. McKagan sighs.
Then we take it
	from the top.

School Dance

Chaperones
(someone else's parents!)
bobbing offbeat

pouring fizzling pink punch
into Styrofoam cups
(but not too much,
since they think we still spill).

Black lights glowing
headless T-shirts
with blue-white teeth.

Kori, Jaleesa, and I
hide in the bathroom,
giggling and glossing,

wondering if
anyone will ever
ask us to dance.

Network

We interrupt this broadcast

to bring you
        the
            late-
                breaking
                    news:

James isn't speaking to Monique
who likes Ivan
whose old girlfriend Sumako
ditched Adam at the dance
and now hangs out with Juan
who dumped LeeAnn
who says Luke and his
twin brother are weird
and still likes Dane,
and *someone* (I'm not saying who)
likes Ryan.

Factoids

Jaleesa collects facts, data tidbits,
reporting that:
> a shark is the only fish
>> that can blink with both eyes,
> a cat has thirty-two muscles
>> in each ear,
> the memory span of a goldfish
>> is three seconds.

I discover a new fact for Jaleesa:
> There are 336 dimples
>> on a regulation golf ball.
Next day, Jaleesa brings a golf ball to school,
> fact-checks, counting
>> every single dimple.

Foreign Language

Jaz is teaching us French.
Lupe is teaching us Spanish.

So far, we can say:
>   *Je suis un petit ballon bleu.*
>   (I am a small blue balloon.)
>   *Me gustan las papas volantes.*
>   (I like flying potatoes.)

We invent other Useful Phrases:
>   *My grandmother lost her big red cow.*
>   *Aliens are swimming in my dog's dish.*

We laugh until our sides ache:
>   Our giggles need no translation.

Thursday

Kori, eating lunch,
acting like she's not wearing
a rubber pig snout.

Does He or Doesn't He?

Kori says I'm smiling funny,
interrogates me,
grills me, until she
forces me to confess
I secretly like Ryan.

We carefully analyze
Ryan's every move,
looking for hints
that he might like me, too.
When it seems he might,
Kori passes a note
to Jaleesa, who gives it to Zach
to pass to Craig,
who gives it to Ryan.

Does he like me?
Well, he kind of does.

Now what?

Worth Hearing

Craig's poem was
magic, much better
than mine.

Craig's turn
to read his poem.
I could tell
he was worried
he might stutter.

He stood up slowly,
his stutter
like the heartache
of a trapped bird,
wings beating
against the windows.

Silently, Craig handed me
his poem.
I stood next to him,
reading slowly
until Craig
found his voice.

Zach's Watch

Zach's new watch
    tells the date,
    position of the sun,
    precise to the second,
    tuned by satellite.

I see Zach explaining
    the features
    of his computerized watch
    to an eighth grader
    who can't be bothered
    to give Zach

    the time of day.

Passing Notes

I dump my backpack,
my notes flutter out.
Hearts, squares, some folded
smaller than my fingertip.
Some arrived
hidden inside markers,
or pinned to pink erasers.
Veterans of covert operations
during language arts,

Top Secret conversations
        scatter silently across the floor.

Much More Flute Practice

After a few notes,
this song seems familiar.
Twinkle little star?

Joan of Arc

Sunday night,
I've finished
a five-page report
on Joan of Arc.
I'm astounded
that a young girl
did what she did,
endured,
died how she did.

Then I stop,
remembering
I'm supposed
to draw a picture.

Joan deserves better
than my stick figures,
lollipop trees.
I take some ashes
from the fireplace,
shudder as I streak
the truth across the page:
Joan at the Stake.

Un-Tied Tongue

Ryan waits for me to say
        Something.
        Anything.
My heart pounds.
Then the words
          s
             p
                i l l
                    o u t .

My un-tied tongue slips,
knots, trips, and tangles.
I knock chotato pips
off the runch loom table.
My mind scrambles
like a gabble scrame,
and I
        even mangle
          his name.

Due Date

1:43 p.m.
heart stops
mental picture:
　　language arts paper
　　five-paragraph essay
　　due today
　　in blue binder

　　　　on kitchen table
　　　　at home.

The Lecture

Mr. Shirling
is giving
The Lecture
again:

Responsibility
Drive & Ambition
Keep Your Nose to
the Grindstone
(Whatever that is.)

Meanwhile,
I am subtly
blowing my nose
to the tune
of
Jingle Bells.

Home Sick

Here I am at home
feeling sick, throwing up,
sipping soda,
a whole day
to myself,
and I'm feeling...

homesick
for school?

That One

Picking up an absence excuse
at the main office,
I overheard something
I wasn't supposed to know,
about the boy who's so tough
the one who scares us so much
the one
who
is coming to school hungry,
sleeping in the garage to hide
from his dad,
who
hasn't seen his mom
in two years.

That one. The tough one.
The one who scares us so much.

Field Trip

The buses are loading
for the field trip.
I grab a window seat, then
Ryan asks me
    if the other
     seat is taken.
All I can do is shake my head.
Kori and Jaz wink, giggle,
kick my seat.

Heading back to school,
Ryan sits next to me
again.
The field trip is a blur.
    Where did we go?
    What did we see?
All I remember
is who was sitting
next to me.

Sunday Night Meltdown

Suddenly remembering
(on Sunday night)
that I have homework
due Monday morning.

The end of my weekend,
like the end of a Popsicle:
instead of one last lick—
a taste of stick.

Science Projects

Steven's doctor-dad
    helped him grow bacteria.
Marta's engineer-mom
    helped her build a radio.
Our parents did nada, zip!—
    while Lupe and I tested
    the effects
    of different
    laundry detergents
    on our dirty socks.

We got an A,
    same as
    the doctor-dad
      and
    engineer-mom.

Free Writing

Ms. Pierson announces
no more grammar,
lights a candle,
turns off the light.
We can write
whatever we want.

I write and write.
When the bell rings
I can't believe I had

so much on my mind.

Growth and Development

Spring again.

Got to remember
        to bring back
            the permission slip
                to watch *that* movie

(you know which movie I mean).

Lupe, Sumako, Kori, and I snicker,
        slump in our chairs,
            stare at our desks,
                then peek to see
                if anyone else
                is *really* watching
                that movie.

Spring Sparrows

Sitting in sixth period,
Kori and I count
twenty-three sparrows
perched on the telephone line,
arranged in a tidy row

f a c i n g *s o u t h.*

Then along comes one more.
They shove each other, *Move over!*
Shuffling shoulder to shoulder,
making room for the twenty-fourth,

who *insists* that he has to sit
in the middle

f a c i n g *n o r t h.*

P.E. Lockers

Brittany and I
    were next-door
    locker neighbors.

She's been gone
    for a month now.
    No one knows why
or where
she went.

I open her locker door,
    empty inside—
    empty, except
for her
lucky socks.

Third from the left,
    fourth row—
    Where did you go?

Band Concert

Bright lights,
dry mouth,
stiff fingers,
insides shaking.

Mr. McKagan
lifts his baton.
I hold my breath,
there's a hush
in the audience.

Then Mr. McKagan
smiles at all of us,
stirs our music,
and we sound
    just right,
    just like
    a real band.

Giggles

Stifle it!
>Ms. Pierson hisses at me.

I can't stop
>nearly doubled up,
>giggles bubbling up,
>contagious
>bounding around the room
>infecting everyone,
>something even funnier
>at each turn.

I get them
>under control,
>then Kori starts
>and I'm off
>on another round.

Ms. Pierson finally gives up, grins, and says,

>*Only seventeen more days of school.*

Award Assembly

Hot auditorium,
principal reading
name after name
of award winners.

I end the suspense
awarding myself

First Place
&
Most Improved
in
Everything
That Matters to Me

Best of all, Margo wins
a Good Citizenship Award
and I clap until
my hands hurt.

Yearbook

Sumako

So glad I got to know you better.

Kori

Friends forever!

Zach

How come you never got trash duty?

Jaleesa

*Did you know that an ostrich's eye
is bigger than its brain?*

Lupe

Stay sweet!

Jaz

Tu es mon amie.

Mr. McKagan

Keep practicing!

Craig

Keep writing.

Ryan

*Toot your flute,
it's summer!*

Last Day of School

Textbooks turned in,
backpacks empty.
Homeroom is just
an empty classroom.

I can't believe it's over.
I survived my first year
of Middle School.
Summer is finally here.

Walking down the steps,
Kori on one side,
Ryan on the other,
laughing, making plans,

suddenly realizing
that Ryan and I
are holding hands,

and I am shining
from the inside out.

More poetry by Kristine O'Connell George

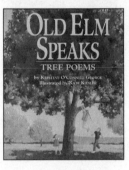

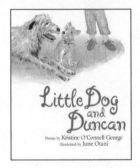